Thirteen Ways
of looking at
the
Highlands
and more

Colin Will

diehard

diehard
publishers
3 Spittal Street
Edinburgh
EH3 9DY

ISBN 0 946230 48 X
© Colin Will 1996

British Library Cataloguing in Publication Data
A catalog record for this book is
available from the British Library

The Publisher acknowledges the financial assistance of the
Scottish Arts Council in the publication of this volume.

27/8/96

The Author is grateful to Sophia Fraser, Robin Yates and
the Arvon Foundation at Moniack Mhor, for providing
peace, support and sustenance in inspirational surroundings,
and to Tessa Ransford and Ruth Padel for suggestions and
encouragement.

Contents

A Taste of Fish

Husbanding volition in the dark pool,
mouthing and gill-gushing water,
tasting chemical memories
from the birthplace spring,
the home-tang of an imprinting riffle,
the hen salmon's programmed need proceeds.

Over fear she forces the fall upward,
tail-strokes levered by pink muscles,
flinging her body in a froth-skimming arc
to slither over the lip's slimed slabs
and flicker through the slick black surge
of the top-water, into the slack.

In a brutal balance,
body is lost to make movement,
nothing else weighs,
oils emulsify to fill yolk sacs,
bones decalcify, deform,
scales tear from spongy skin,
and in the final finishing
of her blind and battering race
a felt and tasted presence,
a red need beside her, under, round,
bestows a milky blessing on her generation.

Red Runner

Beautifully camouflaged, he thinks,
against the bright sprouting wheat,
the spring fox stalks two knowing rooks.
They wait, and lift, crop-forward
into the wind,
and he tailstreams over the field,
pretending indifference,
to the edging trees
in search of an unready vole.
Fail or kill, the habit hones the skill.

I've seen his relations often;
the dog-fox spinning and leaping
in Calder Wood's new snow,
or the vixen who notes and ignores me,
driven by the imperative
of her cubs' hunger.
I'm an irrelevance in a green jacket;
I unleash no terriers.
Or another, panting on a warm rock,
snapping at bluebottles,
guarding her smelly den among the gorse.

Eyes glow in the headlights
as they stand and look at you,
super-foxing towards them
and too often they are dirty red scraps
flat on the road.

But see him run through the hill's rippling grass
ears up and tongue out,
intent, fixed, on a swerving quest,
or hear a pair yip on a still November night,
and know you've met a light and lively being,
the essence of pursuit,
that pointed face where fear and fierceness fuse.

Buzzard

On a glide, mewing to the high world,
you catch an uplift from a sprucy scarp
and turn, rising.

On the chance an outlying treetop
might hold a nervous meal,
you infold wings, falling and fastering.
Nothing scattered, you laze out again
over the edge.

On a whim you slow,
until the stall flutters your upper flights,
and makes you dip and speed into control.

On song, and just because you can,
you loop, twist at the top
and topple into a swoop.

You liked that.
You do it again.

Oilbirds

(Steatornis caripensis, the Oilbird or Devilbird, lives in Caribbean caves, uses echo-location, feeds on fruit; until recently its fat fledglings were caught and boiled for their oil)

Trapped in its cave, our beach is *ours* and open.
We fly about, knowing where
a warmed wind makes music
in the high whine of insects we sense
the weight of our fluttering wings.
On the Earth, above our heads,
thin leaves stutter, we feel air
cooling our beaks, we hear
the clatter of branches.
Down here the cheerful twitter
of constant movement.
We know no liquid flutings,
our furtive clicks point our torches.
The softer floor densely echoes an arch
far above, and rustles a thousand wings,
invisible presences, chart pipes and stacks.
Below, light-shy creatures scuttle
over our dead dinings,
or crackle in the branches of ribs of the furred.
Scents come and go, wafting from hidden heaps.
Reds, whites and browns are wasted here.
Caked mud plasters feet and feathers
of the fallen.
We will remember them,
they flickered us into being.

Glen Tarken

A sheep's skull in the burnt heather,
peat cut and mounded for the unshriven grouse,
the fallen rock big as a tenement,
the concrete block-house and spoil-heap,
all jar and disjoint the flow of the glen's sweet line.
Some are here by chance
or nature's random deal of beauty and destruction,
and others imposed by human fiat.
A concrete gutter ensures each stream is caught,
drying the floor of the glen.
The corkscrew waterfall spins a turbine
and spools peaty vortices far out in brown Loch Earn,
denying the flowers, parching the middle heights.
Under the hills, tunnels and shafts unseen
conduct June's meagre trickles
or the drenchings of dreich November evenings.
In distant cities kettles rattle
and heat dissipates through flimsy walls,
while frog spawn silvers in sunny hollow,
one of a line of linked dry bowls
we used to call a stream bed.

Reflections in Loch Etive

The mist slips over the wet and shining slabs
and just fails to meet the mirroring sea;

the Rorschached hills are violins
or Mandelbrot sets, infinitely complex,
forever never quite the same
on either side of a line of light.

We sleep, but when we wake
a breeze has broken the glass
and shards of wind-whipped water lap
around the mottled boulders.
On the crumbling concrete jetty
a seabird unzips its feathery hooks
and opens its wings in hopes
to dry in the damp and drizzly air.

I love this place. Getting here
is a long and lovely journey,
the river frothing green over pink porphyry falls,
but no-one ever stays long – it's no picnic
site – and there's still solitude
either side of a line of cars,
watching the hills breathe,
cuddled by clouds, bereft, briefly,
of civilised concerns,
alive, simply.

The Rusting Place

A wrecked boat in a Luskentyre field,
the culture of abandonment,
detritus of hope. Things are left
where they cease to function.
Roneval's grey bulk shades
the run-down inn at Rodel.
Repair is not worth it
for no-one ever calls,
and guests pass by because it is a ruin.
In Leverburgh the death of ambition
shows on the faces (aspiration means
never wanting to outgrow your neighbours).
Children from another age,
never carefree
in their respectable scratchy suits,
can play, as long as they don't enjoy it
too much.

Self-oppression is the strongest sort;
self-fear, self-doubt, and righteous self-denial,
all self-obsessive pleasures
in which to take
some smug self-satisfaction.

Tarbert was the place of porterage,
where longships were lifted
from Atlantic to Minch,
saving the long trip round.

The Nordic traders are long gone,
replaced by new, energetic,
short-stay shopkeepers.

Once, at Callanish, the people wondered
if their short lives were all there was,
and hand-hefted shapely stones –
rings of hope, lines of faith –
not looking for subsidies or crooked loans.
Stones stay where they're no longer needed;
a memorial here, a cottage wall there,
a place of pilgrimage
with no more pilgrims.

A land is more than a collection of images,
but some suggest the country.
I've come home, still seeing
the green Atlantic baste the beach at Horgaborst,
and meadow flowers around an ancient plough.

Silhouette
(Ben Wyvis)

The swell of the hills
suggests a lying man,
whaleback chest,
the dip to a flattened gut,
a bulbous jut below.
To the west, the deep cleft of his neck
marking a stream's saddle,
a forever-bleeding wound, rain-fed.
Above the scarp of the chin no mouth,
no nose, just cheekbones, forehead,
and empty sockets staring at the whirling stars.

Culloden

On finding a letter from a military surgeon,
* writing from Inverness, after the battle*

Sometimes a hundred men each day would be treated.
Most had 'feavers', some with the bloody flux.
He would bleed them, naturally, and purge them,
experimenting with a new extract of rhubarb,
if he had the time,
but some were stubborn, unrecovering.
Their tongues would blacken and crack;
their lungs might turn to water, but if they died
he diligently measured the fluid.
Think of all that blood, Charlie;
all those tears;
all the aqueous humours that fill a body
or may be shed.
Charlie, your kind were never worth it,
                                        nor ever will be.
"The Town is become infectious
              by reason of dead bodies."

Looking at the ground,
stung by the beauty of the battlefield,
I try to force mourning,
imagining the sad precision of pibroch.
I should feel at home here, in these alien hills,
but race memory's a myth,
as history is mental reconstruction.
Waiting for a lift to the Lowlands,
like Hawkins praying for a recall,
I sit, back to the wind, choking on thistles.
My respects to you and your mad daughter.

Mining Silver

'God's Blessing' ran out too soon.

Where the Silver Bourn flows
                    below Cairnpapple's kist,
Sandy Maund's 'wondrous ore' shone like metal hair,
till Saxon miners clipped it all away
in seven short years.

At Windywa's the minister's flock diminished
and he migrated.
Inside his mine the timbers
    can be squeezed like sponge;
a fat toad squats in an alcove, in the dark,
and round the entrance there are burning nettles.
On the spoil heaps dead hens advertised
nickel, arsenic, and cobalt too – the Devil's metal –
for blessings are seldom wholly Divine.

The dark and stinking muds in tropical lagoons
at Pumpherston, Uphall, Winchburgh,
transformed to coked and calcined oil-shales; voids
to swallow schools (the price of cheap land),
and hideaway shooting galleries
for the Linhouse Water sniffers.

At Knock you're on a wrecked reef,
a fossil black smoker, plundered for profit,
                              like the rest.
From the atoll's stump view
Ochil and Pentland scarps, below, between,
remember coal swamps as you breathe
Polkemmet's brimstone.

West Lothian's an extractor's Paradise;
new holes are easily punched in the Central Belt,
and the folk are so well used to their waste lines
that the Westwood bing's preserved,
                              for Heaven's sake.

By the 'Blessing' shaft, yellow iris flags waggle
in the summer breeze, and there's always
a lark nearby, with his silver flute.
The grasses ripple like the waves of hair,
or fronds in a coral sea.

Four Archaean Days

At Fanagmore, in the sun,
the lochan lay spattered with waterlilies
with flowers like the sparkles on waves.
Scourie's black dykes cut the speckled granulite,
the continent's rim, furthest back in time.

Loch Laxford's round pink islands,
smooth as upturned boats,
close up reveal the riven clefts and caves,
now seabird ledges,
where veins of plastic rock
forged cracks, miles deep,
under the weight of new crust
in the earliest of times.

The seals tread water, noses in the air,
eyes shut against the sun,
or rest on underwater rocks
like sleeping commas on the swell.

Through the waves in Oldshoremore bay,
sand golden in the sun, a school's boat beaches,
water clear and cold and lively,
and adventurers splash ashore; footprints briefly testify
to human presence; a momentary intrusion.
Under the bridge at Laxford
(fiord of the salmon)
the young laird walks,
tweeded beyond utility,
about to part the waters with his carbon fibre rod.

The salmon leap
out of boredom, maybe
in their Summer Isles prison cages.
But Tanera Beag's otter leaves a gift for us –
sea-urchin fragments wreath a fragrant orchid.

We come and go, we take impressions,
                              and our little marks
swirl and vanish in an instant: the rocks bear witness
to gulfs of eternity, mountains of nearly forever.

Heat Strokes

Six days the weight of warmth grew
pressing our chests thin,
stopping our mouths,
tightening our moods.
Twilight promised only a returning sun
and a fat yellow moon
burned late into the sweating darkness.

Soundless flashes through the shutters
woke us to wars fought with light.
The sky became a flickering screen,
but no silent one – cracks and bomb-bursts
banged between valley-walls,
from peak to crag and cloud;
shards of power left violet images
on our closed eyes.

We turned then to each other
and strove with the storm,
as each phased flash strobed our bodies,
exulting in fear and awe,
demanding the thunder's release.

The Legacy

We travelled north, father and son, to climb Suilven.
I thought my forties memories
              might match his nineties visions.
The Assynt hills, in just being, transcended both.
It still shocked me, when,
from the suddenly clearing mists,
an improbable verticality loomed behind Lochinver;
naked grey rock rising from soupy green hummocks.
The hills remain, eroded tusks of sandstone,
washed down from Greenland highlands
                        before the ocean opened.
They lie like upturned ice-breakers,
as if Scotland planned to force the Northwest Passage,
but held back, for aeons, upon a favourable augury.

Later, looking over Loch Maree to Slioch
I remember a pine marten stopping in the road.
It paused in the grassy mid-line
and stared at our Austin Seven
with our little post-war family.
My father drove on past traffic jams of sheep,
leaving a relict wonder
which has lasted over forty years.

Every father should leave his children mountains –
have Suilven, son. I still have mine.

Glen Turret

The bird
bulleted down the gully,
just over our heads–
peregrine, clearly.
Later, ring ouzels clacked
among the clattering talus;
wheatears heralded along the track;
young hares, hunkered, mileposted our way.
Even grey skies, here,
where we walked,
were light enough – the sun's shaft,
searchlighting the bowl of the glen,
an unnecessary benison.

Beecraigs

In the hills, where we walk
like theme park extras –
the beards, the green jackets,
the "Grand day" greetings–
the monarch of the glen stands,
munching his silage
but still impressive in the glaur,
unaware of market forces.
I feed mints to the hinds
and then buy venison.

Badgers root under spruce
and grebes bring weed
to their foam-fringed platform.
Up the road,
by the limestone mines,
a wildcat emerges from a hole
and kills a cynic.

Tides

Walking far out in the clear green sea,
watching waves at eye height
just that little bit further,
I begin to fear, not being overcome,
but losing, for no reason,
the urge to resist letting go.

Opening Gambit

Dawn's the finest time there is.
I can't fault it, clear or clouded,
it's somehow always novel,
watching skies open towards a sunrise
behind the hills, or pinkening
the city's castle- and spire-lines.
Heaven knows I've seen enough of them,
but there's always the hope
of life becoming brighter
in the hour of the world's lightening.

Calder Wood

This year the whitebeams
looked clotted with snowballs,
and the blackthorn peppered
with cottonwool.
Below the butterbur
bright bugles bluemed.
Crosswort buds were clenched
Christmas chains before unfolding.
By the stream a doe's white scut flashed
as she breasted the bracken,
and a heron, caught rook-robbing,
escaped in a ponderous panic
from the black rags' wrath.

Another egg-stealer cut his foot in the stream
and talked about tetanus.
I should have felt pity
but anger surprised me.
Bloodied stones, darker than campions,
marked the route through the trees,
and broken blackbird shells
showed paler than speedwells
under the whitebeam's branches.

Would smell as sweet
(for Jo)

You said you couldn't write a poem
without a plant name in it.

I know the feeling.

Tonight I wanted to write about love
but 'tormentil' jumped onto the page.
It's a wee yellow constant underfoot;
uncrushable, springing back and spreading, shy
and almost overlookable;
a store of hidden star-gold
strewn through the hill's turf.

I'll come back to love another thyme.
(Damn.)

Parental contribution

I drove to the airport,
through the night,
for his first big lone adventure.
Watching him walk through the gate,
not looking back,
not saying goodbye, hiding feelings,
I thought how grown he was
and how much still my child.
I wanted to hug him
but he'd have hated that then.
I hoped he knew the thought was there, though.

He returned, eyes opened by American road sunrises,
backstreet breakfasts, Greyhound-grown,
Grand Canyon-confident, Chicago-shaken,
an adult.

You don't launch a ship with a push,
you take away the props,
and let its own gravity slide it
into its proper element.

The Forecast
(for Jane)

The wind will howl at the opened window;
the pilgrims at the city's gates will cry;
the clouds will rise so high and heavy
that new tree leaves will glow pale green
against the thunder-grey sunlit sky.

The hail will batter the tops of the mountains;
the people in the streets will dance and sing;
the trees which last year horses chewed
will brown and wither, sway and fall
in a future denied anchorage in the past.

The rivers will trickle on Tuesdays
and flood on the following,
forcing boulders on boulders, sand on sand;
the roads will fill with horses
fleeing the lightning and the thrashing branches.

The sea will wait, weed coils swirling slickly,
then heave froth heavenward over the rocks
and suck back pebbles from the bank
cracking the road, reclaiming the border,
as the birds wheel over uncovering salty pastures.

I will still be here, still,
constant in my centre,
you in my core, and I in yours,
no better calming needed,
no livelier partner in life's several storms.

Twenty-Shilling Wood

I'm sitting, under the first prickle of stars,
poking the coals, turning silver potatoes,
swallowing red wine and wafted monoxide.

Cars pass down the site road,
drivers waving with 'mad bugger' smiles,
red lights tailing to cosy suppers
in chummy restaurants.
I'm not jealous: *this* is where *I* happen, I'm happy
outside my thin-shelled weekend shelter.

I'll stay here, warmly coated,
collar swerving rain-flecked blasts aside;
the charcoal's heat vaporising tree-drips
with a puff of ashes.
Soon I'll slap rosemary'd lamb
on the grill, the sizzling sweet fat
blistering the spitting fire.

The drifting pace of fire-cooking suits me;
it's part of my caravan-calming ritual.

Late rook flights, bat-company mothing round the lights,
and sudden furtive scuffles in the ferns;
the working week past
                    smokes into the night's cleansing air.
Behind me, in the van, comforting ignored noises
of my family and its trivial skirmishing.

I drive here in citied tension, as fast as I can
until, rounding one downhill bend,
the hills' fractal skyline comes into view;
known but new on every now.

This is one of autumn's certain ceremonies.
As leaves ungreen in October's urgency
my barbecue begets a cutting of anxiety;
the season becomes a fall into leafless ease.

Dark 'Ness

Black water hurries between evenly-sloped banks.
Gold and silver lines
rule the river with a metric of lit ripples,
establishing the current's rapid argument
through the bridge's gold-haloed "O".
Giggling gulls blemish the stony shallows
and young folk shoogle the footbridge,
laughing in steamy gusts,
overtaking with jokes.
An oystercatcher tries
to winkle the moon from its dark surround,
passing harrowing overhead –
it's a far cry –
and up in the hills the grave grouse prays
"Go back, go back, go back."

We can't.

Aux Temps

In the pale, autumn light
a high-speed merganser preens downstream,
hurtling, with each backward head-roll
towards its take-off point,
neck at stretch, head and hooked beak fish-ward;
to gamble, double-blind, with the odds of capture.
No guarantees, that's the way of it,
just an unreasoning certainty
we might call faith.

We came back
to flesh a sketchy past,
but found now sufficient
to overwrite memory.

Because we once stood here,
we stand again, thirty years on, stream-stirred,
swept on life's one-way current,
fishing for visions,
rafted on the past,
warmed and proofed by a love
started in shyness, throwing stones,
a stone's throw down from Ness bridge.
We've caught up with our futures.

Thirteen Ways of Looking
at the Highlands

Sub-index

Thirteen Ways of Looking
at the Highlands

Prologue

Too often lately
the birds of anxiety
have anticipated my clockwork waker
in the hours before the light.

From the choked rattle of magpies
to the blackbird's stuttered shriek,
the country is staccatoed with warnings.

In the high here,
where hills unroll to valley floors
and rivers push against the salmon's flow,
the trees and meadows
cherish nests of worry,
egged with anger and with fear.

As a Game

Seen from the Drumochter road
the sheep are grey blebs against the heather
on patchwork tongues of Monadhliath muir-burn.
From ash and stumps grow
green grouse-islands,
then merging carpets
writhe into senescent straggles
and the heather's fiery climax.

All this, for little deaths in feathers.

First draw and pluck your birds
Then hang them for as long as you dare.
Roast simply, and serve on toast,
Soaked in their own juices,
With a little rowan jelly
And game chips.

This, for your stylish diner
in his Highland Theme hotel.

The shooting guests are Land-Rovered
on the higher tracks
for the day's sport,
and at the end the local school-kids,
                              sweaty beaters,
pocket their pittance
and share the ride back
with the keepers,
who much prefer their dogs.

Locals aim their cars
at each strutting pheasant.
Feathers absorb the impact
without marking the bonnet
or disrupting the game.
Spring birds are slowest,
the hen heavy with unshelled embryos
and as you draw the bird you see
there's no future in it.

Spruced Up

For three weeks one winter
the old bird sat in the pine boughs,
scaring the golfers on his third green,
threatening with his bass burp,
head up, neck stretched,
and solid, hooked beak.

        A good thing you taste of turpentine,
        old Capercaillie,
        for You'd furnish a feast.

He's a guzzler of pine needles,
not caring if they're Caledonian remnant
or the token scattering, larch-edged,
where the bonny purple heather
marches with the even green spruce.

Reluctant to face what's in the wood's interior,
along identical anonymous tracks,
unable to see the skyline,
only the lie of the land,
I tread lightly, just inside the forest's skin.
The click of twigs announces
something's here before me,
maybe just behind the windthrow,
or over the rise of ice-smoothed rock
necklaced with the lichen's red gems.

In the wood's silent centre –
a sparse stand of stunted pines –
piles of roe deer's pointed-lozenge droppings lie;
from a bog pool a sheep's spine
forms a bony ladder for a newt,
sphagnum-sliding to the next pond,
passing the coltsfoot's orange-centred sunburst.

Over the fence there's a clear-felled sector,
where scarified soil has washed down
to choke and kill a millennium-old filmy fern
on its soaking hillside.

Trees don't just fall in the woods; I'm haunted,
remembering how my cousin and his family
were log-rolled out of existence
in their car, by an overloaded lorry.
A three-coffin funeral, and a wrecked fourth life,
were too high a price for me to pay for pulp.

The next time Birnam's new tubed wood moves,
the three old women of the wildwood
will cry again to the unworthy:
   To the one-eyed Thane of Selfishness:
   The many-handed Thane of Greed,
   And the death-defying Thane of Ambition,
to realise the profits of the market
and kill the land, the only king.

Rocking and rolling

On a high crag the peregrine chick
screams his hunger to the winds
which lift his wings
   closer to take-off time
with each grouse brought home to roost.

The cliffs circle piles of broken stone,
unsold slates and chippings, at Ballachulish.
Slabbed benches glisten after rain,
bared rock angled just enough for safety,
but too steep to sustain growth,
ledges too smooth
to retain dust or seeds
to green this grey immensity.
As well try to cultivate
the north-east face of Ben Nevis,
or Sron na Ciche's gabbro gauntness.

There are many lesser roadside cauldrons,
now furnished and foliaged homes
for butterfly and bee,
kestrelled with vantages,
where all that was taken
was what was needed
for the next stretch of road, a wall,
or the local kilns. Machinery moved
or rusted into coloured stains.

Mining is a surgical operation
below the skin of the earth,
and the Highland's metamorphic carapace
conceals few lodes,
but hush-gutters cut and scar Beinn Dubhchraig,
and the Foss mine's barite tailings
gleam in their green surrounds.
These burrowings, and their spoil,
are no more than rabbits' work
in the time of a landscape,
and weather will correct, erase.

the bigger gouges
  – "Super" Quarries –
are on a natural scale – as big as nature.
There is, no question, a beauty in barrenness;
we can delight in desolation, for its difference,
but to make it so demands
a quantum hop of arrogance.

To see a hill as money
is not to see a hill.

Beached

Wood anemones in an open field
bear witness to a wood's demise,
but left ungrazed the meadow commune
will reassert itself from dormant seed.

Upland grasslands nourish variety;
pink orchids spike the wetter pastures,
and on the spring flushes
asphodels splay their yellow stars.

Over the beach-grasses of the machair
a corncrake incessants in the thrift,
 behind his tone wall.
The shell-sand drains fiercely,
so roots spread wide
to catch each summer shower.
The trampling tourist herds
or the udder-splayed feet of cows
destroy the network,
leaving brown patches
which coalesce in ruts
of dried flowers,
and sandy paths to beaches.
We'll bag our spot with towels
and all the paraphernalia we take
to remind ourselves

We're at the Sea-Side!

Black-headed gulls,
on a break from the sewage patrol,
land beside our tempting salmonella scraps,
terns yark and splash for sand-eels in the shallows,
and eiders on the waves
bob heads and "Ooh",
outraged by the new best-seller
we're trying to get to grips with
behind our windbreak.

The sand still gets everywhere,
and every year there's more of it,
and less of the green sea-barrier.

Scenic and Cynical

Martins and swallows return each spring
to find their sand-holes and eave-cups,
and that's the time the city folk
start to fantasise a happy isolation
where a circlet of blue-hazed hills
balms a sunny glen,
and a white beach near Durness
becomes an Oasis, for parched
and chip-starved caravanners.
How long before the Smoo Cave
is renamed "Cambrian Park",
with anachronistic dinosaurs
and wee cavemen in tartan loincloths?

How to fleece the sheepish tourists:

> See our Black House
> Where we live on mud floors,
> Discover fossil fish at Achanarass Quarry
> With our Hugh Miller projection;
> Fall before redcoats and renegades at Culloden;
> Make terrorised leaps at Killiecrankie
> (and most other Highland river-narrows);
> Stroll fear-free with animatronic wolves
> and bears:
> See caged gamebirds in the Perthshire hills,
> before they're shot:
> Weave bolts of seriously scratchy cloth
> On genuine reproduction wood-like looms,
> Before you see us all massacred at Glencoe.

This is us, this is how we live.
And to remember us, we suggest
You buy a wee hairy mini-kilted doll, or a tea-caddie –
        (Tea was the national drink of the Picts
        – a little-known factette).
Or how's about a real authentic
Highland-crystal and Caithness-flag
Combined digital thermometer and radio?
It comes engraved with a verse of Burns
On the side, from "To a neep" or
"The Cottar's Saturday Night and Sunday Morning."

   "There's ne'er a bonnie burd that sings
    But minds me o' my gin."

Brings tears to the eyes. A tip?
How unexpected! God Bless You Sir!

If tartanization spreads,
The Highland Experience™
will be the Highland way of life

Holding the Scales

Norway's fjord-cliffs brought back
'our' sea-eagles,
skimming the surface-fish.
Salmon and sea-trout,
smooth sides blemished by the white
scars of sea-lice, bodies curved
to the tail's swift flick,
splashing from salt to fresh
where Morar's water mixes with the sea,
or shore-lining Loch Ailort,
passing their caged and pelleted relatives,
cosseted, chemical-coated,
fatted and coloured,
feted in the supermart's display
with perfect silver skins.

The eagle perches on a power-line
by the shore,
keen eyes mesmerised
by the unreachable maelstrom
of turning fish, netted,
but not yet landed.
In estuaries, fixed nets
strain their tidal take.

Both easy ways
to make meat
to make money, unless Norway
dumps the prey
as it hands us the predator.

Inland, the heron's down-curved wings
cup air with each heavy measured flap
as it breasts the wind.
In the dam's delayed waters
trout flash at the surface,
attracting the buzzard's spiral stoop,
or the osprey's surface-skimming flop.

Anglers admire and curse,
jealous of their rival's success,
upset that human craft and cunning
are so easily matched and bettered
by the natural skills
of the winged fish-hunters.

Caught or harvested, poor fish,
you pay the price
for being bloodless, non-sentient,
                    and tasty.
Everyone's after you,
even the urban bourgeous vegetarians,
for although all animal flesh is meat,
they use a fashionable sophistry
to class you fair, with fowl,
and feed on you.

Safe as Houses

Serviced plots for sale are strung out
along the scenically stunning roads.
The Inverkirkaig single-track
from Lochinver to Suilven
is a linear village:
weekender cottages and neat wee
ranch-style bungalows abound;
strings of white dots you tear along
in the awesome bleakness.

Caravans parked in birch woods
each have neat fenced borders
where gnomes abuse the primulas,
and the bubbling of chaffinches,
                welcoming newcomers,
in reality's a scrap-happy cheerfulness.
On misted mornings dainty deer
step from the trees to nibble
the Garden Centre's imported delicacies.

The affluent put on the Highlands
like a labelled accessory
they'll soon park
with the Barbours and the wellies.
The country's here to serve them
                and they to accept service.
There are more houses
than people to live in them,
but the monied buy the places
where the locals can't afford to live.

Imported cats plague the blackbirds,
enjoying the careful stalk
on a trusting fledgling,
claw-punching until the red drops
elicit the final bite.
This, your house-cat,
bringing death to the suburbs
as the suburbs burgeon.

The remotest glens each have their lodges,
their 'Keep Out' signs proclaiming ownership
of blocks of beauty
bigger than cities.
King's gifts, parcelled debts paid
to supportive barons,
              sold on, sold out.
Then , as now, the unasked inhabitants
had no say in how they were to live.
The voice of the deer is unheeded,
as irrelevant as the crofter's squeal of pain.
Trusteeship, governance, the common good,
are concepts not weighed
in an accountant's balance,
so count for nothing.

With the Jet Set

Trainee killers scream low up the glen
shielded by radar and head-up displays
from the scared sheep below
and the shivering, skinny-dipping tourist.
A millionaire lifestyle
to bomb the foe
'Back to the Stone Age.'

The jet-scream is one thing,
and soon frights are forgotten,
but why are they here? Who asked them?
Does the military own the air
over our heads?
They lob bombs in the sea
off Cape Wrath, whose huge cliffs,
    Sites of Special Reproductive Significance
for gannets and guillemots, become
    Sights, Natural, Bomb-Aimers for the Use of.
Too much of our land is Off Limits
to the people who should own it.
We need defending against
The Ministry of Defence.

Faslane sterilised a coastline,
and before it the Holy Loch
spread its nuclear tentacles
into its hinterland.

        Beware the beasts in Glen Fruin,
            and Glen Douglas!

Bunkered MIRV warheads make certain
this beauty-ground
is ground zero for a pre-emptive strike,
but from where? From whom?
Who would want us? A small nation
on the ragged edge of Europe, endowed
with haggis and scones.

At Aultbea the convoy escorts assembled,
and the rusting concrete still nests
below gneiss-bouldered slopes.
Fortifications ring the coastline,
forestalling Hitler's landing
planned for Broughty Ferry,
of Napoleon's invasion of Bonahaven.
Dunottar Castle frightened off Genghis Kahn,
or we'd have had Mongol horsemen
clattering down the Waverley Steppes.
Newer European raiders, and their money,
are welcome, although some B & B's
still repel boarders.

As each warplane passes –
I ask myself – "One of ours?
Or one of theirs?
Which is which?
And who would know?"
All swords are double-edged,
                    but so are shields.

Sheepishly

The strangely silent struggles
of an upturned sheep
flagging its feet
like burned match-heads
excused inaction in the onlooker.
If you'd screamed pain
or bellowed fear,
I'd have braved the barbed wire
and the embarrassment,
and helped you
          maybe.

Siblings grazed close, ignoring you.
The whole day you lay there,
and the long wet night which followed,
thin belly – fell chilled by the wind,
until the next morning
you were hauled upright
by rough, caring hands.
The hoodie waiting on the fence-post
flew away. "Keep your eyes
in this field, there are still enough
undevoured afterbirths."

Enclosed sheep, in fields, are fine;
they can go on sharing
with rabbits and gorse,
juniper and orchids;
it's their cousins in the hills I mind,

stripping the wild flowers.
shearing each seedling tree,
until only an odd rock-rooted rowan
escapes their relentless teeth.

Heavy-boled trees grew here,
renewing oaks made timber for homes,
birch flames roasted meat and barley,
and the hot ash branches fired the kilns
for pots and beakers, as bronze
smelted in the bag-bellowed ovens.

But the forests were mown
for charcoal furnaces
charged with bog-iron ore.
Then the human crop of the glens
was dispersed for wool futures
and the silent clearing
which took grandmother's side to Buchan
and grandfather's to the Black Isle,
and then to the 'soft' south's tenements.

My ancestry's strung out on the map,
in little lights – mostly red.
Mutches and Wills sparkle
in Dingwall and Tain,
Peterhead and Aberdeen
Clan Gunn? Strath Uille?
The lights are out.

In the Shit

A pair of goldfinch flashed red and yellow
on the thistle-stalks, amid the smell
of drying sewage.

The river's flood plain made a convenience
for 'Environmental Health' (Ha!)
to discharge waste untreated,
sure of a fast flow to the disguising sea,
but after the fall
shreds and solids clung to tree-branch
and herb-stem. Turds returned,
and insanitary odours
made their presents felt –
a bonus for the waterbirds –
gull-heaven for the blackheads
screaming their baleful challenges,
and a pleasant change of diet
for pigeons used to pecking vomit
and carry-outs from village pavements.

Round the coast the caravan sites
deliver their piped detritus
to a sea whose fathomed pebbles
were once clearly seen,
Mermaid's purses, rare cast-ups
on spring beaches, are outnumbered
by their latex look-alikes,
and moon-cycle remnants
float among the wracked crab-pools.

There's destruction in heat too,
where cooling water forces algal growth
sieved by oysters and mussels,
made noxious by their harboured toxins,
or bloats the streams
with brown festoons
which capture oxygen
in exchange for stink.

Off the fields, nitrates and phosphates leach
their poisonous excess,
accelerating growth with water-weed,
concentrating death in the tissues of fishes
and sterilising fish-eaters
far to sea;
storing malformations, cancers, teratogens,
nerve-poisons.

  "What would you like on your fish supper?"

"Salt, vinegar, cadmium, mercury, oestrogens,
                    organometallics, acid rain."

All the contentious condiments
of this filthy age.

As a Green Place for Deer

Struggling for breath,
bearing your townie's fat and lethargy,
you step by step get higher.
Pause for a gasp and a view
on the shoulder before
the next steep grass pitch,
and listen, through the wind's engine,
to a conversational croak overhead.

The ravens break off
soaring and tumbling
in the cliff's updraught
to see what new struggler
has entered their defended patch
of hillside.

Yesterday, it was the deer descending,
beset by blood-biters.
Emerging maggots dropped like special offers
from their twitching flanks
and lungworms were sneezed to the grass
in the warm low grounds.
The herds are too heavy for their pasture,
culling costs too high.
The heights are grazed back to the peat,
to the bitter heather, bald rock-pates
and stone-choked streams.

Roadside fields near tourist roads
have their token Highland cattle,
    all hair, and horn, and shitty tails,
and their de-antlered herds
of farmed venison.

Putting wolves back in the hills
would add a certain *frisson* to a mountain hike
and put the wind up bikers,
and a glimpse of lynx in the birch-woods
would be a fine hair-raising thing,
but I don't think we'd appreciate
bears browsing our tart little blueberries
with their bloomed black skins.
    They'd clear the glens faster
than the lairds of Sutherland.
The real fear would be
that wolves would find lamb-slaughter
easier than stalking deer,
and a Wolf reserve would exclude people
more easily than 'Firing Range' notices.

The sad fact is,
that the last mangy wolf
shot in the Highlands
lived in a different age.

We can't unwind time
and pretend that nothing else
would change.

On the Skids

Ptarmigan peck for wind-blown seeds
on the snow's crust,
observing as fact, without judgement,
the tracks of the skiers
    rutting the downslopes,
    cutting the earthskin,
    crushing the high meadow's quilt.

The summer scars split hillsides
into straight-edged patches;
fresh brown lines follow
the shortest route from top to bottom
and the water follows,
widening and steepening the fissure,
stripping soil faster than the ice could grind
to bare ski-shaping rock:
so the sterile zone widens.

Improve access, double the tows
and lifts, until the hillsides are criss-cross
with lines,
    a giant scratching-post
    for city man's
    technological itches.

Climbing the Devil's Staircase
above Kinlochleven
we were forced to stop
as mountain-bikers exercised
their might-of-way.
        Village streets are lined
        with manacled bicycles.

It won't be long before
their richer, thicker cousins
start ploughing the tracks
with off-road vehicles.

The hills, it seems, are for exercise –
take Ben Cruachan for a good brisk walk,
        (fine chap, Ben)
or race Stuc a'Chroin to the summit
and slide back down
the In-Pin's edge.

        (Eagles once seen over the Buachaille
        grew to pterodactyl size
        before their suspended human prey
        identified hang gliders
        defending Glen Coe.)

Bright and shiny clothes,
the right wax, and length of runners apart,
Highland skiing is a downhill business.

Summarily

The birds whirl over the land,
skyring up crags
and skiting on downdraughts.
They'll pick and choose
which of our novelties
suit them. They'll be changed by them,
as citied pigeons have been,
and suburban-suited blackbirds,
insured and future-proofed
by garden shrubbery,
as homely as any woodland understorey.

The deer will crash
from predation or hunger,
scalping the hilltops,
raiding fields in winter,
competing with geese
to set the stage for the next
shotgun stand-off.

The military will always find new toys
to keep their wee boys happy,
castling their sand-pies
while the rooks laugh.

Cheaper sunshine elsewhere
will beacon the tourists
fleeing the midges, the mists,
and the optimally-drenching drizzle.

And if our scenery's passé
and our theme parks strike no chords
just think – who else if not the Scots
could give the world McDonalds?

You don't need the eyes of an owl
to intimate wisdom,
and to see in the dark
is to miss most of what's there.
Let's switch on the light of reason
and see which way Scotland's headed;
let's decide if the Highlands –
a Victorian invention –
were ever part of this ending century;
let's hold this upland vastness
as all Scotland's heritage
entrusted for the next Millennium.

Epilogue

Towards evening,
at the end of a week's writing,
the haze lifted and clear air entered.
The snow tonguing Ben Wyvis' flanks,
and nippling the Monar hills,
restored perspective
with Highland healing.

Somehow, in remoteness and altitude,
solitude and ruggedness,
we each bring *our own* Highlands home.
It's enough.

There's a blackbird nesting in my firethorn;
four fat chicks will inherit the garden
and sing me awake.

COLIN WILL

Dr Colin Will, Librarian of the Royal Botanic Gardens, Edinburgh, and previously Librarian of the British Geological Survey, has been writing environmental poems about the Highlands and Natural History, and indeed poems in a wider context, for many years. He has published his poems both in literary journals and in the scientific and environmental literature, and even in mountaineering journals! He has also provided poems for exhibitions in his capacity as Librarian of the Royal Botanic Gardens.

Colin's involvement with writing goes further than this — he often gives poetry readings, plays saxophone in poetry and jazz, and has set up and led workshops and seminars on writing and botany. He is a member of the Committee of the Scottish Poetry Library.

other diehard poetry

Richard Livermore **The Divine Joker** 0 946230 24 2 £3.60
   *"Distinctive titles...The anarchic goddess who figures in most of
   these poems works well as a device to let Richard Livermore be deadly
   serious and have fun at the same time"* – Books in Scotland

Sally Evans **Millennial or, the Far Side of English**
   0 946230 22 6 £6 *long poem. "Often passages delight with the sheer
   rightness of their humour and versification"* – Acumen
   "A considerable achievement" – Iron

Martha Modena Vertreace **Light Caught Bending** 0 946230 285
   £4.50 *"Widely praised because of the range and depth of ideas behind
   her poems"* M. Bugeja, The Art and craft of Poetry. *"The poems all
   sparkle with originality and are a great pleasure to read"* – NHI

Tony Rees **The Rhondda Sonnets** 0 946230 24 2 £2 *lovely little
   pamphlet of sonnets in English - and they don't mention coal even
   once!*

poetry related

Joy Hendry **Gang Doun wi a Sang** a play about William Soutar
   0 946230 25 0 £5 *"There must be a warm welcome for its first
   appearance in print ... a fine introduction to the Perth poet."*

Bill Dunlop **Klytemnestra's Bairns** 0 946230 21 8 £4.50
   *a dramatisation of Aeschylus' Oresteia in Scots verse. "The Scots
   language brings an immortal play deeper within our most intimate
   selves"* – The Scotsman

John Cargill Thompson **What Shakespeare Missed** 0 946230 30 7
   £4.50 *3 plays; includes The Marvellous Boy, a play about Thomas
   Chatterton first presented at 1994 Edinburgh Fringe Festival.*